You're One of a

A Children's Book about Human Uniqueness

by

Joy Wilt

Illustrated by Ernie Hergenroeder

Educational Products Division
Word, Incorporated
Waco, Texas

Author

JOY WILT is creator and director of Children's Ministries, an organization that provides resources "for people who care about children"—speakers, workshops, demonstrations, consulting services, and training institutes. A certified elementary school teacher, administrator, and early childhood specialist, Joy is also consultant to and professor in the master's degree program in children's ministries for Fuller Theological Seminary. Joy is a graduate of LaVerne College, LaVerne, California (B.A. in Biological Science), and Pacific Oaks College, Pasadena, California (M.A. in Human Development). She is author of three books, *Happily Ever After, An Uncomplicated Guide to Becoming a Superparent,* and *Taming the Big Bad Wolves,* as well as the popular *Can-Make-And-Do Books.* Joy's commitment "never to forget what it feels like to be a child" permeates the many innovative programs she has developed and her work as lecturer, consultant, writer, and—not least—mother of two children, Christopher and Lisa.

Artist

ERNIE HERGENROEDER is founder and owner of Hergie & Associates (a visual communications studio and advertising agency). With the establishment of this company in 1975, "Hergie" and his wife, Faith, settled in San Jose with their four children, Lynn, Kathy, Stephen, and Beth. Active in community and church affairs, Hergie is involved in presenting creative workshops for teachers, ministers, and others who wish to understand the techniques of communicating visually. He also lectures in high schools to encourage young artists toward a career in commercial art. Hergie serves as a consultant to organizations such as the Police Athletic League (PAL), Girl Scouts, and religious and secular corporations. His ultimate goal is to touch the hearts of kids (8 to 80) all over the world—visually!

Contents

Introduction

You're One of a Kind is one of a series of books. The complete set is called *Ready-Set-Grow!*

You're One of a Kind deals with human uniqueness and can be used by itself or as part of a program that utilizes all of the *Ready-Set-Grow!* books.

You're One of a Kind is specifically designed for children ages four to eight. Children can either read the book themselves or have it read to them. This can be done at home, church, or school.

You're One of a Kind is designed to involve children in the concepts being taught. This is done by simply and carefully explaining each concept and then asking questions that invite a response from the child. It is hoped that by answering the questions the child will personalize the concept and, thus, integrate it into his or her thinking.

Much has been written about the importance of each child having a positive self-concept, but very little has been said about how a positive self-concept can be developed.

If children are to think well of themselves, they must realize and accept the fact that they are human beings — persons.

Once they have grasped this concept, they can begin to understand that because they are persons, they are unique — "one of a kind."

This can be redeeming for children because they are going through a stage of life in which they frown upon being different. Most children have an overwhelming desire to be exactly like everyone else in their group. When children discover that they are different — and that being different is normal and acceptable — they begin to accept themselves. When they discover that being different is desirable, they can begin to value themselves.

You're One of a Kind is designed to teach children that each person is unique and that uniqueness is normal, acceptable, and desirable. This book is also designed to teach a child that when God created him or her, God did not make any mistakes. Everything God does has a purpose and fits into a total plan. "Being unique" is part of God's plan for every human being. Children who grow up believing and accepting this will be equipped to live healthy, exciting lives.

You're One of a Kind

You're one of a kind.

Do you know what it means to be one of a kind?

If you do not know what it means to be one of a kind, that's O K because . . .

this book will tell you all about it.

What does it mean to be one of a kind?

CHAPTER 1

Every Person has a One·of·a·Kind Body

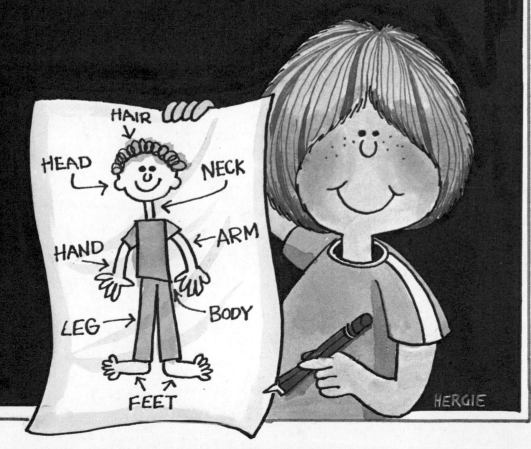

This is Lisa. Lisa is seven years old. Lisa is a person.

Lisa has a one-of-a-kind body.

17

Lisa has . . .

frog

blue eyes, brown hair, and a cute nose
with freckles on it.

Lisa also has . . .

twenty-four teeth with a little
space between her two front teeth.

Lisa is . . .

fifty inches tall.

20

Lisa weighs . . .

fifty-five pounds.

Lisa wears . . .

a size eight dress.

Lisa also wears . . .

size one shoes.

It is true there may be a lot of seven-
year-old girls who have

—blue eyes

—brown hair

—a cute nose with freckles on it

—twenty-four teeth with a space
between the two front ones

—a body that is fifty inches tall

—a body that weighs fifty-five pounds

—a body that wears a size eight dress

—feet that wear size one shoes.

But . . .

No other person has a head, a body, arms, hands, legs, and feet that are shaped . . .

. . . exactly like Lisa's. Every person has a body-shape that is not like any other person's.

No other person has handprints or fingerprints . . .

. . . exactly like Lisa's. Every person has handprints
and fingerprints that are not like any other person's.

No other person has footprints . . .

. . . exactly like Lisa's. Every person
has footprints that are not like any
other person's.

No other person has hair . . .

. . . exactly like Lisa's. Every person
has hair that is not like any other
person's.

No other person has teeth . . .

. . . exactly like Lisa's. Every person has teeth that are not like any other person's.

31

No other person even smells . . .

. . . exactly like Lisa. Every person has an odor that is not like any other person's.

All of these things:

Lisa's eyes
Lisa's hair
Lisa's facial features
Lisa's teeth
Lisa's height
Lisa's weight
Lisa's dress size
Lisa's shoe size
Lisa's body-shape
Lisa's handprints
Lisa's fingerprints
Lisa's footprints
Lisa's odor

make Lisa's body one of a kind.

Lisa's body is
one of a kind because
no other person has a
body exactly
like Lisa's.

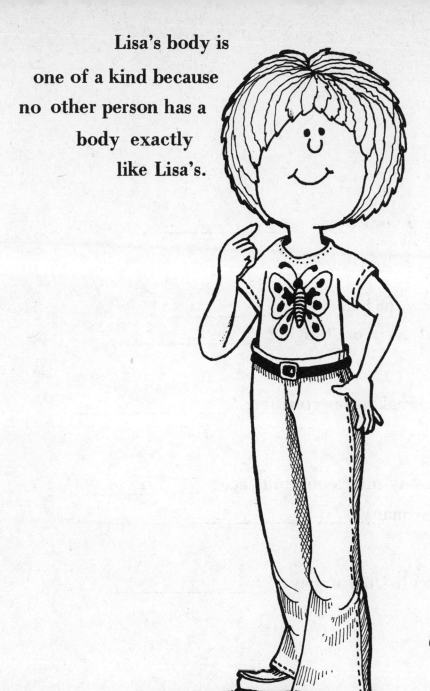

God created Lisa's body
one of a kind.

What color are your eyes? _____

What color is your hair? _____
      Is it curly or straight? _____

Do you have freckles on your face? _____

Do you have any moles on your face? _____
      How many? _____

How many teeth do you have? _____

Paste a photograph or draw a picture of your head on this page.

How tall are you? _____

How much do you weigh? _____

What size shoes do you wear? _____

What size clothes do you wear? _____

Paste a photograph or draw a picture of your body on this page.

Use an ink pad to make your fingerprints or
draw your handprint on this page.

Use an ink pad to make your toeprints or
draw part of your footprint on this page.

All of these things:

your eyes
your hair
your facial features
your teeth
your height
your weight
your clothes size
your shoe size
your body-shape
your handprints
your footprints
your odor

make your body one of a kind.

Your body is one of a kind because no
other person has a body exactly like yours!

God created your body one of a kind.

What does it mean to be one of a kind?

CHAPTER 2

Every Person has a One-of-a-Kind Personality

This is Kristen. Kristen is six years old.   Kristen is a person.

Kristen has a
one-of-a-kind personality.

47

Kristen likes . . .

the color yellow,

strawberry
ice cream,

kittens,

4-square,

bike riding,

and

Disneyland.

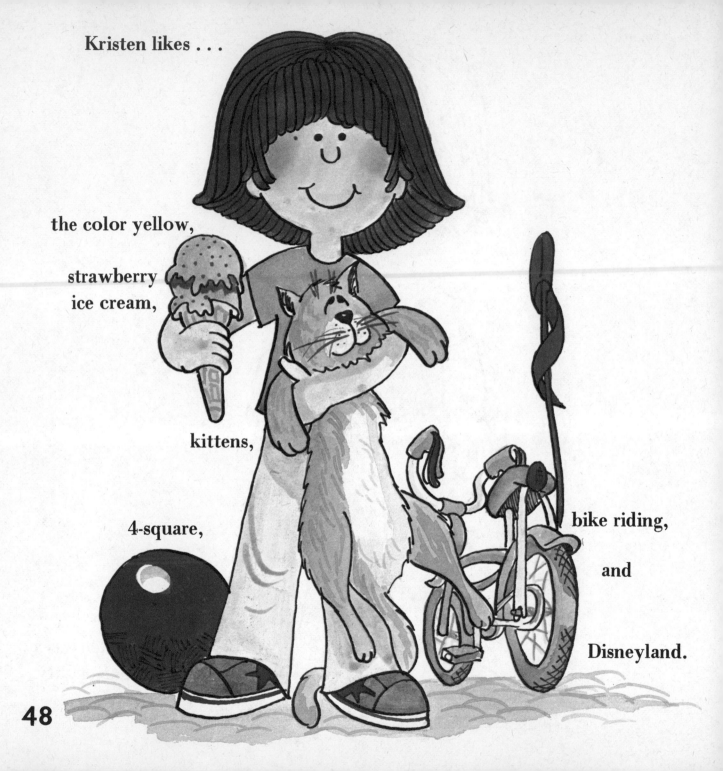

48

Kristen does not like . . .

the color brown,

waiting in long lines,

snakes,

pickles,

tetherball,

or

going to the doctor.

Kristen is interested in . . .

reading,
writing,
spelling,
and language.

ARITHMETIC IS ICKY

Kristen is not interested in . . .

arithmetic, science, and social studies.

51

Kristen believes . . .

the Tooth Fairy,

the Easter Bunny,

and Santa Claus

are real.

52

Kristen does not believe that . . .

ghosts,

goblins,

and
monsters

are real. **53**

Kristen thinks . . .

that her teacher this year
is fabulous!

Kristen thinks . . .

that her teacher last year
wasn't so hot!

Kristen thinks . . .

that practical jokes

(tricks played on people)

are not funny.

Kristen thinks . . .

that jokes and riddles are funny.

When Kristen is mad . . .

she stamps her feet and screams.

When Kristen is sad . . .

SNIFF

she cries and wants to
be by herself.

When Kristen is with a lot of people . . .

she is shy and does not want to talk very much.

When Kristen is with her family, or with one or two of her best friends . . .

she is not shy and loves to talk.

Kristen is good . . .

at art and making things.

Kristen is not very good . . .

at singing and dancing.

Kristen has a good habit . . .

of brushing her teeth two
times a day.

Kristen has a bad habit . . .

of biting her nails.

Kristen does not usually . . .

finish what she starts or   do what she says she will do.

Kristen is . . .

messy instead of neat, and
slow at doing things instead of fast.

All of these things:

what Kristen likes
what Kristen is interested in
what Kristen believes
what Kristen thinks
what makes Kristen laugh
how Kristen shows her feelings
how Kristen feels and acts around other people
what Kristen is good and not good at doing
what Kristen's good and bad habits are
whether or not Kristen does what she says she will do
whether Kristen is a hard worker or lazy
whether Kristen is neat or messy
whether Kristen does things quickly or slowly

make Kristen's personality one of a kind.

Kristen's personality is
one of a kind because
no other person has a
personality exactly
like Kristen's.

God created
Kristen's personality
one of a kind.

What don't you like to eat? _____

What do you like to eat? _____

What games do you like to play? _____

What games do you not like to play? _____

Color these squares the colors that you like.

Color these circles the colors that you don't like.

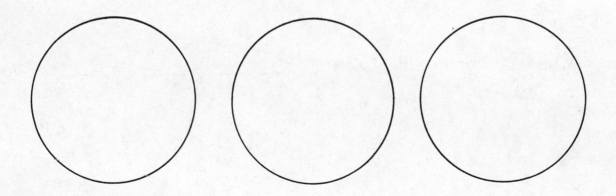

What do you like to do? _____

What do you not like to do? _____

Where do you like to go? _____

Where do you not like to go? _____

On the top half of this page draw a picture of an animal you like.

On the bottom of this page draw a picture of an animal you don't like.

Do you believe in . . .

	YES	NO
Santa Claus?		
Easter Bunny?		
Tooth Fairy?		
Sandman?		
Monsters?		
Ghosts?		
Goblins?		

74

Are you interested in . . .

	YES	NO
Reading?		
Writing?		
Spelling?		
Language?		
Arithmetic?		
Science?		
Social Studies?		

What do you think about . . .

	Yucky	OK	Fantastic
Your Doctor?			
Your Teacher?			
Your Dentist?			
Your Neighbor?			
Your Neighborhood?			
Your School?			
Your Church?			

Draw a picture of yourself laughing.

What makes you laugh the most? _____

_____

_____ **77**

What do you do when you get mad? _____

What do you do when you are sad? _____

What do you do when you are happy? _____

What do you do when you are excited? _____

Do you like being with people, or would
you rather be alone? _____

Circle the group that you would rather be with.

A Lot of People   A Few Friends

What are you good at doing? _____

What are you not good at doing? _____

What are your good habits? _____

What are your bad habits? _____

	YES	NO
Do you usually finish the things you start?		
Do you do what you say you will do?		
Are you a hard worker or are you lazy?		
Are you neat or are you messy?		
Do you do things quickly or do you do them slowly?		

All of these things:

what you like
what you are interested in
what you believe
what you think
what makes you laugh
how you show your feelings
how you feel and act around other people
what you are good and what you are not good at doing
what your good and bad habits are
whether or not you do what you say you will do
whether you are a hard worker or lazy
whether you are neat or messy
whether you do things quickly or slowly

make your personality one of a kind.

Your personality is one of a kind because
no other person has a personality exactly
like yours.

God created your personality one of a kind.

What does it mean to be one of a kind?

CHAPTER 3

Every Person has a
One · of · a · Kind Situation

This is Chris. Chris is six years old.   Chris is a person.

Chris has a
one-of-a-kind situation.

Chris lives in a house . . . that has three bedrooms, a kitchen, a bathroom, a living room, and a medium-sized backyard.

Chris lives with his family . . .

a mother, a father, an older brother, an older sister, and a younger sister.

Chris' family has several pets . . .

a dog, a cat, a bird,
a goldfish,
and a mouse.

Chris' family has a car . . .

a station wagon.

Chris has four grandparents . . .

two grandmothers and two grandfathers.

three aunts, two uncles, and five cousins.

Chris goes to school . . .

at an elementary school.

Chris goes to church . . .

at a community church.

Chris has two best friends . . .

one is a girl, and one is a boy.

Chris has one enemy . . .

a nine-year-old boy.

Chris takes piano lessons . . .

once a week.

One time Chris had to go
to the hospital . . .

to get stitches.

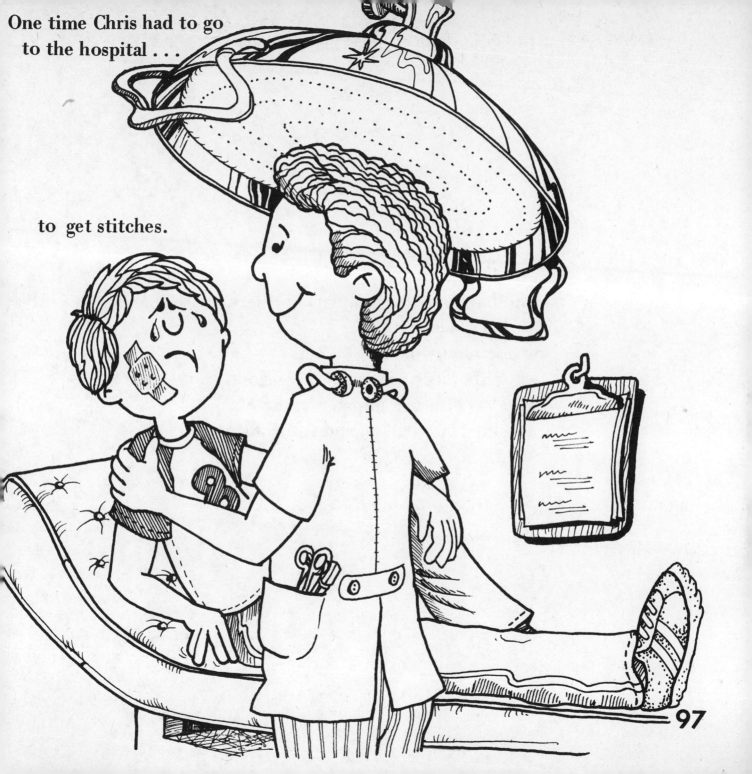

It is true there may be a lot of boys and girls

who live in a house
who have a mother, father, brothers,
    and sisters
whose family has several pets
whose family owns a station wagon
who have four grandparents, three
    aunts, two uncles, and five cousins

who go to an elementary school
who go to a community church
who have two best friends
who have one enemy
who have gone to the hospital to
get stitches.

But . . .

It is Chris . . .

who has a mother named Millie, a father named Harold, an older brother named Robbie, an older sister named Nancy, and a younger sister named Tina.

It is Chris' family . . .

who has a cat named Rhoda,
a basset hound named Ralph,
a parakeet named Chirpie,
a goldfish named Carrot,
and a mouse named
Pipsqueak.

It is Chris' family . . .

who owns the station wagon with a

dented rear fender.

It is Chris . . .

who has grandmothers named Grandma Mary and Grandma Alice
and grandfathers named Grandpa Pete and Grandpa Joe.

It is Chris . . .

who has aunts named Aunt Sally, Aunt Ann, and Aunt Katie; uncles named
Uncle Rick, Uncle Don, and Uncle Cal; and cousins named Maria, Sue, Laura,
David, and Joel.

It is Chris . . .

who goes to Pleasant Town
Elementary School.

It is Chris . . .

who goes to Pleasant Town
Community Church.

It is Chris . . .

who has a best friend named
Sarah and a best friend named Randy.

It is Chris . . .

who has an enemy named Seymour.

It is Chris . . .

who takes piano lessons from

Miss Snogenberger.

It is Chris . . .

who had to get six stitches in his head because he got hit by a wild pitch while playing in a Little League game.

All these things:

where Chris lives
what family Chris lives with
what Chris' family has
who Chris' relatives are
where Chris goes to school
where Chris goes to church
who Chris' friends are
who Chris' enemies are
what Chris does
what happens to Chris

make Chris' situation one of a kind.

Chris' situation is one of a kind because no other person has a situation exactly like Chris'.

God created Chris and allows him to be in a situation that is one of a kind.

Where do you live? _____

How many people are in your family? _____

What are their names? _____

How many pets live at your house? _____

What are their names? _____

Does your family have a car? _____

What kind? _____

Paste a photograph or draw a picture of your family and pets on this page.

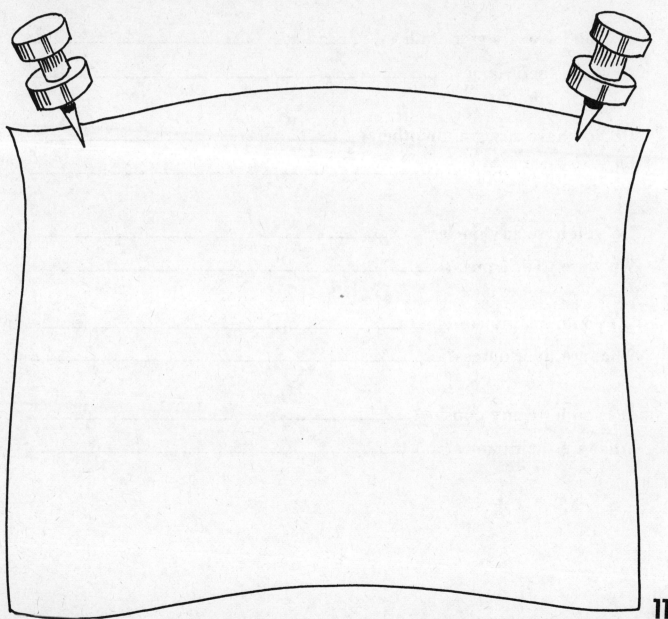

Do you have any grandfathers? _____

What are their names? _____

Do you have any grandmothers? _____

What are their names? _____

Do you have any uncles? _____

What are their names? _____

Do you have any aunts? _____

What are their names? _____

Do you have any cousins? _____

What are their names? _____

Do you go to school? If so, where?_____

What grade are you in?_____

Who is your teacher?_____

What are some things you do at your school? _____

Where do you go to church?_____

What class are you in?_____

Who is your teacher?_____

What are some things you do at your church?_____

_____

Do you have any best friends? _____

_____

Who are they? _____

_____

Do you have any enemies? _____

_____

Who are they? _____

_____

Paste a photograph or draw pictures showing some things you do or places you go during your free time.

Write about or draw a picture of the most terrible thing that happened to you.

Write about or draw a picture of the most exciting thing that happened to you.

All these things:

where you live
what family you live with
what your family has
who your relatives are
where you go to school
where you go to church
who your friends are
who your enemies are
what you do
what happens to you

make your situation one of a kind.

Your situation is one of a kind because no other person has a situation exactly like yours!

God created you and allows you to be in a situation that is one of a kind.

So what does it mean to be one of a kind?

CONCLUSION

You're one of a kind.

You have a body that is not like any other person's.

You have a personality that is not like any other person's.

You have a situation that is not like any other person's.

And . . .

God created your body unlike any other person's.

God created your personality unlike any other person's.

God allows you to be in a situation
    that is not like any other person's.

So, that makes you . . .

ONE OF A KIND

He's very valuable because no one else is
like him and he could never be replaced.